Gudrun Rogge-Wiest

Nevertheless be Free

A literary Journey

Essays I

For

Johanna and Clara

Tristam and Yuliya

Bibliografische Information der Deutschen Nationalbibliothek:
Die Deutsche Nationalbibliothek verzeichnet diese Publikation
in der Deutschen Nationalbibliografie; detaillierte bibliografische Daten
sind im Internet über dnb.dnb.de abrufbar.

© 2020 Gudrun Rogge-Wiest
Herstellung und Verlag:
BoD – Books on Demand, Norderstedt

ISBN: 9783751951791

Contents

I

II

Preface

Nevertheless be Free is a collection of essays about literary texts. The chosen extracts, the poems and the film lead the way on a literary journey with freedom as its guiding theme.

They are not new discoveries, but favourite pieces, classics in the sense that it is worth returning to them in order to read them in the light of present-day reality and, inversely, to take them as a frame of reference illumining aspects of life in our own times. Accordingly, they have inspired me to observe myself and my surroundings more consciously.

The authors created their works in response to the life of their times, its vicissitudes and fault lines and passed down to us, their readers, what they distilled from their impressions. The protagonists and speaker personae face situations that are in essence familiar to us despite the temporal distance. We can put ourselves in their shoes, reflect on their emotions, thoughts and behaviour, and relate them to our own experiences.

Simultaneously the works deal with timeless questions of human life. How are signs or situations interpreted, how decisions made? What is the role of the individual in society and how is freedom possible? Thus, readers can bridge the time gap and enter into a conversation with the work.

As most of the cited texts were originally written in German, this book also provides an opportunity to get in touch with some important German literary works and their authors.

The chapters contain analyses of the cited pieces in the sense of a close reading, supplemented by references to their biographical or socio-political contexts. They conclude with a glance at how they can relate to human experience today.

Though the footnotes may sometimes seem too bulky for the page, I decided not to abridge them, because they are a valuable component of the work. They are meant to be a treasure trove for further reading and study.

More than any other occupation, reading books makes it possible to fade out one's everyday life and to become familiar with other though not entirely dissimilar worlds in order to view one's own in a different light. In this spirit the curtain opens for the first chapter.

I

And nevertheless be free - *Sansibar*
or The Last Reason

Then he became aware [...] of the presence of the figure. It was sitting on a low metal plinth at the foot of the pillar diagonally opposite. It was carved from wood, which was neither light nor dark but simply brown. Gregor approached it. The figure represented a young man reading in a book that was lying on his knees. The young man wore a long garment, a monk's garment, no, a garment which was even plainer than that of a monk: a long gown. Under the gown his naked feet protruded. His two arms were hanging down. His hair, too, was hanging down straight on both sides of his forehead covering his ears and his temples. [...]

How old is he? As old as we were when we read just so. Eighteen, no more than eighteen. Gregor bent down lower in order to be able to see the young man's face properly. He bears our face, he thought, the face of our youth, the face of the youth chosen to read the texts that matter. But then he noticed suddenly that the young man was completely different. He was not rapt. He was not even absorbed in his reading. What was it he was doing? He was quite simply reading. He was reading attentively. He was reading precisely. He was even reading with the utmost concentration. But he was reading critically. He looked as if he knew at each and every moment what it was that he was reading. His arms were hanging down, but they seemed ready to carry a finger to the text at any moment which would point out: this is not true. I don´t believe this. He is different, thought Gregor, he is completely different. He is lighter than we were, more birdlike. He looks like someone who can close his book at any time and get up to do something entirely different.

So is he not reading one of his holy texts, thought Gregor. So is he not like a young monk? Is this possible: being a young monk and not being overawed by the texts? Taking orders and nevertheless be free? Living by the rules without subduing the spirit?

Gregor stood up. He was confused. He observed the young man who continued reading as if nothing had happened. But something happened, thought Gregor. I have seen someone who lives without a mission. Someone who can read but who can still get up and go. He looked at the figure with a kind of envy.

Alfred Andersch, *Sansibar oder der letzte Grund*. Diogenes Verlag 1972. Extract from 'Gregor' (42-45).

Gregor, a communist party functionary, perceives in the sculpture of a young reading monk his own younger self, the student of the Lenin Academy in Moscow[1], who

---

[1] The Lenin Academy was the training centre of the Comintern (Communist International), the international association of communist parties.

devotedly absorbs the teachings offered to him. On closer examination, however, he notices a crucial difference. While he identified with the content of his books as a student, the sculpture represents an independent-minded reader who concentrates on his texts on the one hand, but at the same time keeps his distance and thus has the option to disagree with them, to question their teachings. Thus he can protect himself against being manipulated. Composure and a sense of humour, which the observer perceives in the corners of the monk's eyes, help to uphold such a stance of inner freedom. [2]

These reflections on the sculpture of the young monk have the character of a moment of awakening for Gregor through which he gets his bearings and finds his purpose. As a young man he dedicated his life to the communist party not unlike a monk. Now he is on a mission

---

[2] The German sculptor Ernst Barlach's work *Lesender Klosterschüler (Young Reading Monk)* 1930 was the model for Andersch's sculpture. A photo can be found on www.landesmuseum-mecklenburg.de/exponate/Ernst-Barlach-Stiftung-Guestrow/ernst-barlach-lesender-klosterschueler/.

to organize resistance against the Nazi regime among the party members in Germany. Even before his encounter with the sculpture Gregor daydreamed of a possible flight from Nazi Germany and from the communist party mainly because he was scared, but also because he needed some space to find out what his own position was.

> *And I, what do I want? I want to escape from my corner and go anywhere, to a place where you can think [...], think about if it still makes sense to believe in the party. (49)*

With his own experience of alienation from the communist party in mind, he immediately understands why the Nazis are keen on making the figure disappear from public view. An invitation to reading and thinking critically could not be in their interest, because this would lead to doubts about their ideology and their rule.[3] Thus, the reading monk becomes an allegory of independent

---

[3] Immanuel Kant famously defined Enlightenment as independent thinking leading to the liberation of the individual. 'Answering the Question: What Is Enlightenment?' (German *'Beantwortung der Frage: Was ist Aufklärung?'*) Berlinische Monatsschrift, Dezember 1784)

thinking and by implication a symbol of resistance against 'the Others', the author's term for supporters of the National Socialist Party.[4] Gregor understands that by rescuing the sculpture the stance it represents will be preserved for the new era after their rule. Due to the significance he attributes to this enterprise, he is willing to put his life on the line in order to achieve the new purpose, which he has found for himself.[5]

---

[4] Cp. the definitions in Jeremy Tambling, *Allegory*, London [u.a.]: Routledge, 2009. 'I will, in order to present personification, assume throughout that it is an allegorical mode, providing concrete forms for complex, abstract ideas which it makes recognizable.' Tambling, 5.and '[…] personification, which like prosopopoeia, ascribes a mask, or face, and by implication a voice and personality, to an object or something in nature, or even to a man-made object, such as a statue (43).

[5] Erich Fromm distinguishes this kind of sacrifice from the one the Nazi's glorified: 'It is one of the tragic facts of life that the demands of our physical self and the aims of our mental self can conflict; that actually we may have to sacrifice our physical self in order to assert the integrity of our spiritual self .This sacrifice will never lose its tragic quality. Death is never sweet, not even if it is suffered for the highest ideal. It remains unspeakably bitter, and still it can be the utmost assertion of our individuality. Such sacrifice is fundamentally different from the 'sacrifice' which Fascism preaches. There, sacrifice is not the highest price man may have to pay to assert his self, but it is an aim in itself. This masochistic sacrifice sees the fulfilment of life in its very negation, in the annihilation of the self. It is only the supreme expression of what Fascism aims at in all its ramifications--the annihilation of the individual self and its utter submission to a higher power.' *The Fear of Freedom*, chapter 7, 'Freedom and Democracy', 231.

In the description of the monk's way of reading the term attentiveness takes central place. The critical reader approaches the text with an open mind, is both thorough and alert.

Critical reading can be taken as far as to be deconstructionist, that is, according to the manner described by deconstructionism, a postmodernist method of literary studies. While reading 'against the grain', deconstructionism always takes the text as a point of reference.[6] Therefore, it is not a licence for arbitrariness or for criticism in the service of a world view or some vested interest. Instead, proper deconstructionists outline their method and reflect their points of view as all other good researchers do. A well-founded deconstructionist analysis leads to replicable findings and insights.

---

[6] A good introduction is the chapter 'Structuralism and post-structuralism-some practical differences' in Barry, Peter *Beginning theory. An introduction to literary and cultural theory*, Manchester and New York: Manchester University Press, 2002

In the light of today's heated public debates, it takes a great effort to *nevertheless be free* (*trotzdem frei bleiben*). It can also be made an ideal with regard to our understanding of the world around us, the world as the text we read and interpret every day. The sculpture of the reading monk can remind us to stop and think *without subduing the spirit* (*ohne den Geist zu binden*) in order to be able to form our own opinion.

II

Magical artefacts – *The Chamber of Secrets*

In a girls' bathroom, which is out of order because it is often flooded, Harry Potter finds a diary. Once he is on his own, he examines it. In order to make it respond he writes in it, and in reply, writing appears on the page.[7] The writer introduces himself as Tom Riddle. In the course of the ensuing written conversation Tom Riddle tries to make Harry believe that Hagrid opened the Chamber of Secrets fifty years earlier and let out the deadly Basilisk.

Harry does not let himself be led on because he knows Hagrid well and trusts him absolutely. Thus, Harry does not fall prey to Tom Riddle. Ron Weasley's little sister, Jinny, however, does. The story of how Tom Riddle's diary affects her reads like a psychological case study on seduction and manipulation.

---

[7] Joanne K. Rowling, *Chamber of Secrets*, 'The Very Secret Diary', London: Bloomsbury, 2014, 254.

It is the death eater Lucius Malfoy, who passes the book on to Jinny in the jostle of the crowded bookshop in Diagon Alley in London. When she starts using it, she is vulnerable, because it is her first year at Hogwarts, and she is lonely. Tom Riddle, alias Voldemort, engages in a conversation with her until she becomes emotionally dependent on his sympathy and understanding. Finally, he makes her open the chamber of secrets despite her initial reluctance, thereby exposing the residents of Hogwarts to great danger. Jinny is unable to free herself from Riddle's influence by her own effort. Her tentative attempts to communicate her plight fail, not least because the people she turns to, only slightly older than herself, do not really take her seriously.

In subsequent Harry Potter volumes Tom Riddle's diary is occasionally cited as a warning, that it is essential to identify the creator of a magical object and to find out about their affiliation before engaging with it further. Witches and wizards are taught this rule by responsible parents such as the Weasleys at a young age (348). They make their children aware that it is vital to make sure that an object does not contain dark magic or is even associated with the death eaters around Voldemort.

Time and again, it is evident that the warning is justified and that 'constant watchfulness' is not the precept of alarmists. So Ron's rat Scabbers turns out to be Wormtail, Voldemort's most faithful servant, in disguise (*The Prisoner of Azkaban*) and images of Sirius lying on the floor of a corridor in the basement of the Ministry of Magic transmitted to Harry through his access to Voldemort's mind prove to be a trap (*The Order of the Phoenix*). All these cases illustrate that it's easier said than done to just live by the rules. Life is so complex that it can be impossible to realize where danger really lurks and to make the right decision.

The psychology of seduction illustrated by Jinny Weasley's story can also be observed in the virtual reality of the internet. The repercussions range from gaming addiction to gambling addiction, from political manipulation to radicalization.[8] Though school children today are taught from an early age that it is important to have some essential information on the source of a text, be it a news article or just a message on Facebook or Twitter, in order to be able to evaluate whether it is trustworthy or not, a large number of children and adolescents have fallen into a trap. Their experience confirms the importance of being sceptical and not to let oneself be carried away.

---

[8] Radicalization is encouraged by websites of Islamist and right-wing extremist groupings. Manipulations of the will of the electorate occurred in the run-up both to the Brexit referendum and the Presidential elections in the US in 2016.

III

When winter comes – 'Half of life'

Hälfte des Lebens

Mit gelben Birnen hänget
Und voll mit wilden Rosen
Das Land in den See,
Ihr holden Schwäne,
Und trunken von Küssen
Tunkt ihr das Haupt
Ins heilignüchterne Wasser.

Weh mir, wo nehm ich, wenn
Es Winter ist, die Blumen, und wo
Den Sonnenschein,
Und Schatten der Erde ?
Die Mauern stehn
Sprachlos und kalt, im Winde
Klirren die Fahnen.

Friedrich Hölderlin (1804)

Half of life

The land with yellow pears
And full of wild roses
Hangs into the lake.
Oh, gracious swans,
And drunk with kisses,
You plunge your heads
Into the wholly pure water.

Alas, for where in winter
Can I get the flowers and where
the sunlight
and shadows of the earth?
The walls stand
speechless and cold, the wind
jangles the weathervanes.

Friedrich Hölderlin (1804)[9]

---

[9] The translation is by David Constantine, with slight adaptations informed by Ulrich Knoop's interpretation of the poem in ‚Hälfte des Lebens', Wortgeschichtliche Erläuterungen zu Hölderlins Gedicht' ['Half of Life', On the Etymology of Words in Hölderlin's poem] on www.ulrich-knoop.com/hölderlin/hälfte-des-lebens/, 1999-2007

The speaker is surrounded by the richness and fertility of a beautiful late summer's day. It finds powerful expression in the interplay of land, water and living beings. The thought of winter, however, brings about a sudden change of mood. The image of a dystopian landscape rises to the surface of his consciousness, bleak, without life and beauty and dominated by cold, speechless walls. Dread and horror make him utter a cry of woe.

The title 'Hälfte des Lebens' ('Half of Life') indicates that the two landscapes evoked in the poem are representative of human experience.[10] To the present-day reader they seem to point to the ages of man. The fear of old age makes itself felt even in one's prime. An unknown and ineluctable destiny lies ahead, and only death is certain.

---

[10] I would like to remind my readers that I do not aspire to the high standards of scholarship in this essay. Readers of German can find an excellent interpretation by Ulrich Knoop, which is based on the contemporary use of words and Hölderlin's thinking (Ulrich Knoop, 1999-2007). My translation of 'heilig' into 'Into the wholly pure water' in verse 7, for example, is based on Knoop's findings.

Alternatively the two landscapes might stand for contrasting states of mind, a time of joy that alternates with a depressive mood. The transition can occur with or without a specific stimulus. Even during a good time the artist – the swan is a symbol of the poet – might be overcome by fear of his creativity running dry.[11]

The sequence of the seasons from late summer to winter suggests that winter will in its turn be followed by spring. However, there is not a glimpse of this.[12] Instead, the poem ends on a jarring note which resonates beyond the last line. It seems that once you have had such an apocalyptic vision, it is hardly possible to return to lightheartedness.

The contrast between abundance and bleakness, wellbeing and horror seems to have been a hallmark of human life throughout its history until today. Western liberal societies today seem to offer a foretaste of paradise

---

[11] Ulrich Knoop, 1999-2007.
[12] It should be noted that in Hölderlin´s system of thought winter is the time dedicated to creativity (Knoop, 1999- 2007).

for the middle class. They live in freedom and relative prosperity, their rights are protected and there is some social welfare, but this state of affairs is kept up by exploitation of workers in our own countries and above all in the low-wage countries of Asia and Africa. Besides, it can be observed in the living conditions of animals in factory farming and in the treatment of nature everywhere on earth. Though we consumers receive images of the resulting misery, we are able to ignore them while living our crowded everyday lives. We deal in a similar way with the consequences of climate change largely brought about by greenhouse gas emissions of the industrial nations. Shortages of water and food, drought and floods threaten the existence of people above all in the poorer nations. We live in a paradise of illusions.

It was in the autumn of 2018 that Hölderlin's poem was constantly with me. On my walks through orchards with their trees full of fruit and each day as warm and sunny as the next one, it seemed like being in paradise.

And yet, behind the heart-warming beauty dangers were lying in wait. Agreeable as the warm October sun was, it triggered memories of the heat wave and the lack of rain in the previous summer, the brown fields in the Rhine valley and in north eastern Germany, the poor corn and vegetable harvests.

The season also reminded me of the previous year when the trees hardly bore any fruit, because of a late period of frost in the spring of 2017 destroying the blossoms on the fruit trees. It was a scary sight. These images, whose cause is not a caprice of the weather but progressing climate change, are a foreshadowing of a bleaker reality which that won't spare Western Europe.

While temperatures on Earth are rising, recent tendencies in western liberal societies seem to foreshadow a social winter. Hatred and agitation have made room for themselves in the public debate, and they are fuelled by precarious jobs, poverty, hopelessness and a growing gap between rich and poor. This has led to alienation with as yet unforeseeable consequences.

In the wealthier milieus of western societies like in Hölderlin's poem the fullness of life is still the reality, but the horror scenario looms on the horizon.

IV

Stormy times – 'All Enshrouded in Grey Clouds'

Eingehüllt in graue Wolken

Eingehüllt in graue Wolken,
Schlafen jetzt die großen Götter,
Und ich höre, wie sie schnarchen,
Und wir haben wildes Wetter.

Wildes Wetter! Sturmeswüten
Will das arme Schiff zerschellen -
Ach, wer zügelt diese Winde
Und die herrenlosen Wellen!

Kanns nicht hindern, daß es stürmet,
Daß da dröhnen Mast und Bretter,
Und ich hüll mich in den Mantel,
Um zu schlafen wie die Götter.

Heinrich Heine, *Nachgelesene Gedichte* (1812-27)

Enshrouded in Grey Clouds

Enshrouded in grey clouds,
asleep the great gods lie,
I hear them snoring,
and wild weather is upon us.

Wild weather, indeed! - A storm is raging,
willing to blast this poor old ship.
alas, these winds, who 'll rein them in?
and the unbound, masterless waves?

I can't stop the storm from raging,
making boards and masthead boom.
and in my cloak enshroud myself
to sleep just like the gods.

Heinrich Heine, *Nachgelesene Gedichte*
(Weeded-out poems), 1812-27

In Greek mythology the gods live, love and argue like

humans, and what they do or leave undone has an im-

pact on life in the world. In Heine's poem they are

asleep, while a fierce storm is raging. Only they could

pacify the forces of nature by commanding the winds and the waves to lay off, but they are unaware of what is happening. Finally, the speaker follows their example, enshrouds himself in his cloak and lies down to sleep. Thus, he imitates the gods.

This move is expressive of a conscious detachment from the depicted scene. The events represented in the second stanza '[...] A storm is raging,/ set to blast this poor old ship./ alas, these winds [...]' come across as dramatic. The final image of the speaker going to sleep, however, indicates his inner distance and suggests an ironic overtone. It conveys his awareness that there won´t be a miraculous rescue.

Heine´s interest in current affairs suggests an allegorical meaning. After the Congress in Vienna in 1815, the princely rulers of the German states under the predominance of the Austrian Empire basically restored absolute rule and oppressed forces demanding freedom and more rights. With the Carlsbad Decrees of 1819 police powers were extended, and far-reaching censorship was established.[13] The Gods stand for the princes of the early 19th century, the ship corresponds to the contemporary state and the social order it was based on. The storm is a metaphor for the longed-for revolution of the people that was to bring about a more democratic, constitutional German nation state.

On closer examination, there is a crucial difference between relations on the literal level (initial text[14]) - the gods, the ship and the storm - on the one hand and those on the allegorical level - the princes, the social order and the angry people - on the other, which confirms the suspicion of irony created by the speaker going to sleep.

---

[13] Rolf Hosfeld, *Heinrich Heine. Die Erfindung des europäischen Intellektuellen.* München: Siedler Verlag, 2014, 53.

[14] Kurz, Gerhard (1982/2009) *Metapher, Allegorie, Symbol,* Göttingen: Vandenhoeck, 6. Auflage, 44. In this chapter, Kurz explains Quilligan's terminology for the analysis of allegorical texts. She distinguishes between the so-called initial text with its initial meaning and the allegorical interpretation of the text. What the text obviously expresses is its initial meaning, but it also contains clues pointing to an underlying allegorical level. The narrative the reader arrives at by connecting the clues, is his/her allegorical interpretation of the text.

While the gods cannot be dethroned, the princes are not invincible, so they cannot actually afford to sleep, that is, to ignore the protests and postpone necessary reforms indefinitely. Thus the irony implies criticism of these rulers.

Unlike the princes, the speaker does not have any influence on the workings of history ('I can't stop the storm from raging', stanza three), the revolution is going to run its course, anyway. When he enshrouds himself in his coat and lies down, he makes a pretentious gesture. Despite being powerless, he compares himself with the Gods. Even though he remains exposed to the storm, as a commoner the speaker has more liberty than the nobility, which is another ironic discrepancy. On the one hand it points to his vulnerability, on the other hand to the option of at least keeping his composure as a first step to attaining inner freedom and dignity.

We can imagine the speaker to be a persona of the poet himself, who was a keen observer of the political developments in contemporary Germany. Heine wrote in a situation of political oppression. The poem does not refer explicitly to the circumstances, and at first glance the initial text veils the allegorical meaning. However, it can be easily decoded, and the ironic effect conveys the unspoken criticism. Both allegory as the mode of presentation and irony as a poetic device can be pictured as the author's cloak, in which he enshrouds his poem and himself. Both can be considered as defence strategies against the interference of the authorities.[15]

Whereas the poem 'All Enshrouded in Grey Clouds' contains only veiled criticism, Heine did not conceal his

---

[15] The works of Dmitri Shostakovich can be cited as another example of the use of irony in a situation of extreme political oppression (cp. Chapter VI in this essay collection on Pasternak's poem 'Hamlet'. In his fictional biography Julian Barnes writes about the function of irony for the composer: 'All his life he had relied on irony. He imagined that the trait had been born in the usual place. In the gap between how we imagine, or suppose, or hope life will turn out, and the way it actually does. So irony becomes a defence of the self and the soul, it lets you breathe on a day-to-day basis.', *The Noise of Time*, Chapter 3.

political position in many of his other works. These writings were directed against the autocratic policies of the princes of the German Confederation whose repressive measures became even more rigorous after the Hambach Festival of 1832. Their author himself was an advocate of a liberal democratic constitutional state, but he was at the same time critical of radical republicans like Ludwig Börne.[16] Riots against Jews, censorship and the upsurge of anti-liberal Christian forces in Germany finally led him to immigrate to France in 1831, where he lived until the end of his life.[17]

In the wake of the Cholera epidemic of 1832 in France, Heine learned what the consequences of revolution might be for the insurgents, when demonstrations against the July Monarchy were brutally crushed by government troops.[18] As a well-to-do exile, however, who was welcomed in the salons of the upper middle classes,

---

[16] Rolf Hosfeld, *Heinrich Heine.* 278.
[17] Rolf Hosfeld, *Heinrich Heine,* 224-6.
[18] Rolf Hosfeld, *Heinrich Heine,* 272.

he was in a sense enshrouded in a protective coat. On the other hand, by refusing to comply with the prescriptions of the authorities, he exposed himself to attacks by Christian-conservative authors loyal to the regime and ran the risk of his works being banned. While loyalists made a bogeyman out of the French and their country, because it was admired for its liberal-mindedness among the advocates for political change, Heine set out to explain France to the Germans and Germany to the French.

Although he did not hide his political affiliations, he saw himself as an independent artist, who does not actively campaign for a cause.[19] Apart from being a prominent voice of the democratic opposition, Heine was also vulnerable because of his family background. As a Jew he suffered from discrimination as well as from Anti-Semitic insults. He witnessed Anti-Semitic riots both as a youth in his home town of Düsseldorf in 1819 and as an

---

[19] Rolf Hosfeld, *Heinrich Heine.*, 253.

adult in Hamburg in 1830. They were one of his reasons for going into self-imposed exile.

Beyond the historical context the situation outlined in the poem can arise at any time when dissatisfaction with the government grows because they refuse to carry out reforms. As a consequence social tensions build up and protests are likely to erupt. Most recently, a series of incidents of police violence against Afro-Americans has triggered protests against systemic discrimination and racism in the US.

Worldwide the paralysis of governments with regard to the fast-progressing climate change has caused the young generation to stage protests, which found increasing support in the course of 2019. Still, by the beginning of 2020 there were hardly any binding commitments to implement the measures necessary to contain climate change. It is not unlikely that the corona pandemic leads to a further catastrophic postponement of effective action. With regard to climate change governments all over the world are asleep, and too many people do not seem to care much, either or have other priorities. We are in for a rude awakening.

V

Enchantment of the soul with dark consequences – 'The Linden Tree' in *The Magic Mountain*

Der Lindenbaum

Am Brunnen vor dem Tore
Da steht ein Lindenbaum;
Ich träumt in seinem Schatten
So manchen süßen Traum.

Ich schnitt in seine Rinde
So manches liebe Wort.
Es zog in Freud und Leide
Zu ihm mich immer fort.

Ich mußt auch heute wandern
Vorbei in tiefer Nacht,
Da hab ich noch im Dunkel
Die Augen zugemacht.

Und seine Zweige rauschten,
Als riefen sie mir zu:
Komm her zu mir, Geselle
Hier findst du deine Ruh!

Die kalten Winde bliesen
Mir grad ins Angesicht,
Der Hut flog mir vom Kopfe,
Ich wendete mich nicht.

Nun bin ich manche Stunde
Entfernt von jenem Ort,
Und immer hör ich's rauschen:
Du fändest Ruhe dort!

Wilhelm Müller, 1823.[20]

The Linden Tree

At the well before the gate
There stands a linden tree;
I dreamed in its shade
Quite a few sweet dreams

I cut into its bark
Quite a few words of love
I was in joy and sorrow
Drawn back to it time and again.

[20] *Deutsche Gedichte. Eine Anthologie.* Reclam, 2002, 171.

Today I had to wander
Past once more at dead of night,
And even in the dark
I had to close my eyes.

And its branches rustled
As if calling out to me:
Come here to me, old fellow,
Here you´ll find your rest.

The cold winds blew
Straight in my face:
My hat flew off my head.
I did not turn back

Now I am quite some hours
away from that spot;
And still I hear that rustling:
You´d find rest there.[21]

Wilhelm Müller, 1823

---

[21] The main source of this translation is *Schubert´s Winter Journey* by Ian Bostridge. A few turns of phrase are my own. I also drew inspiration from the English translation in *Winterreise. Liederzyklus nach Gedichten von Wilhelm Müller, D911/op.89* (1827), Textbeilage zur Aufnahme mit Dietrich Fischer-Dieskau und Gerald Moore, Deutsche Grammophon, 1972.

A gramophone, a cutting-edge device newly acquired by the management of the Sanatorium Berghof in Davos, where the protagonist Hans Castorp spends seven years, enables the patients to listen to music without a live performance. Hans Castorp's enthrallment is a cue for the narrator to introduce five of his favourite musical pieces, starting from their effect on the protagonist. 'The Linden Tree' is the last and the only German one in this sequence.

Let us put it this way: an object created by the human spirit and intellect, that is, a significant object, is 'significant' in that it points beyond itself, is an expression and exponent of a more universal spirit and intellect, of a whole world of feelings and ideas that have found a more or less perfect image of themselves in that object – by which the degree of its significance is then measured. Moreover, love for such an object is itself equally 'significant.' It says something about the person who feels it, it defines his relationship to the universe, to the world represented by the created object and, whether consciously or unconsciously, loved along with it. [...]

What was this world that stood behind it, which his intuitive scruples told him was a world of forbidden love?

It was death.

But that is sheer madness! A beautiful, marvellous song like that? A pure masterpiece, born out of the profoundest, most sacred depths

of a whole nation's emotions – one of its most precious possessions,
, the archetype of genuine feeling, the very soul of loveliness? What
hateful slander!

Oh my, oh my – that was all very pretty, was what any upright
man would have to day. And yet, behind this sweet, lovely, fair work
of art stood death. It had special ties with death, ties one might in-
deed love, but not without first 'playing king,' not without intui-
tively taking into account a certain illegitimacy in such love. In its
own original being, there may have been no sympathy with death,
only something full of life and folk culture. But to feel spiritual and
intellectual sympathy with it was to feel sympathy with death. In its
beginnings, purest piety, the epitome of pensiveness. There should
be no thought of contesting that. But in its train came the workings
of darkness.

What was all this he had himself believing? He would not have let
any of you talk him out of it. The workings of darkness. Dark work-
ings. Torturers at work, misanthrope dressed in Spanish black with
a starched ruff and with lust in place of love – the outcome of popular
simplicity and devotion. [...]

But what's this? Hans Castorp's sweet, fair, nostalgic song, the
emotional world to which it belonged and his love for that world –
they were supposed to be 'sick'? Not at all. There was nothing more
healthy, more genial on earth. Except that this was a fruit – a fresh,
plump, healthy fruit, that was liable, extraordinarily liable, to begin
to rot and decay at that very moment, or perhaps the next; and alt-
hough it was purest regalement of the spirit when enjoyed at the
right moment, only a moment later and it could spread rot and decay
among those who partook of it. It was a fruit of life, sired by death
and pregnant with death. It was a miracle of the soul – the ultimate

miracle, perhaps, in the eyes of unscrupulous beauty, who gave it her blessing; yet it was regarded with mistrust, and for valid reasons, by the responsible eye of someone 'playing king' and who affirmed life and loved its organic wholeness. Both a miracle and a challenge, which overcome, would be equal to a triumph over himself.

Yes, triumph over self, that may well have been the essence of his triumph over this love – over this enchantment of the soul with dark consequences.

Thomas Mann, *The Magic Mountain*, Translation by John E. Woods [plus some adjustments], New York, Vintage International, 1995, 641-643.[22]

'The Linden Tree' from the lied cycle *Winterreise* bei Franz Schubert[23] is the only one of the musical pieces to stand in the context of the ongoing dispute between Settembrini and Naphta, two philosophically inclined fellow-patients vying for Hans Castorp's attention and

---

[22] For speakers of German I recommend the audio book with Gert Westphal, Audio CD Album *Der Zauberberg* by Deutsche Grammophon. The extract is located at the beginning of CD 14.
[23] D911/op.89 (1827). Schubert set to music the eponymous cycle of poems by Wilhelm Müller (1794-1827).

approval with their contrasting world views. Central aspects are their different conceptions of liberty and truth.

Liberty

Settembrini's ideal is the liberal bourgeois democracy, based on a separation of church and state. Liberty is understood as individual liberty within the boundaries of the rule of law. It is defined and protected by human and civil rights. Conflicts between the individual and society arise when individuals violate social norms and values in their attempt to assert their self-interest or when they have broken the law. (391)

Naphta was born into a Jewish family. As a young man he joined the Catholic order of the Jesuits. He criticizes Settembrini's bourgeois humanism and ridicules social norms and values calling them 'morality' and 'virtuousness' in a pejorative sense. Naphta's utopia is the theocratic state. As the church was founded by God, it takes precedence over the state, despite the apparent contradiction between taking power and the ideal of abnegation. He considers the 'compromise' to be legitimate because it is supposed to be only a temporary arrangement and serves the religious goal.

> *But if the kingdom is to come, the dualism between good and evil, between this world and the next, between power and the Spirit, must be temporarily abrogated and transformed in a principle that unites asceticism and dominion. That is what I call the necessity of terror.'*
> Chapter 6: The City of God and Evil Deliverance, 395.

Naphta's theocracy is equal to a dictatorship, to a tyranny. Its instruments include physical punishment and torture. Liberty is located in the spiritual dimension alone, that is, it is attained by turning away from the affairs of this world. When humans resist the temptations of the sensual and physical, they defeat the devil, who fights with God for their souls (601). Similarly, suffering physical pain is considered as beneficial, as a way to atone for one's sins.[24] Therefore, being seriously ill is a desirable condition and invalids are worshipped.

Human dignity is achieved by subordination and by sacrificing oneself for a higher purpose, be it one's faith, an ideology or the glory of the nation. The security of the individual in a bourgeois life, which Settembrini values, is looked down upon. A painful death in the service of the faith is glorified. Martyrdom is true nobility.

Naphta trusts in the seemingly paradoxical appeal of such a tyranny, especially to the youth.

> *It is ultimately a cruel misunderstanding of youth to believe it will find its heart's desire in freedom. Its deepest desire is to obey. [,…] The mystery and precept of our age is not liberation and development of the ego. What our age needs, what it demands, what it will create for itself, is – terror.'*
> Chapter 6: 'The City of God and Evil Deliverance', 393.
> .

---

[24] This interpretation of physical agony was common in the Middle Ages. It found its expression in acts of self-flagellation among others. 'As early as the 1260s, and especially after the plague of 1348/49, there were flagellant processions all over the [Holy Roman] Empire. The lay people taking part in these processions carried out ritualized self-flagellations in order to atone for their sins and to follow the example of Jesus Christ.' Source: www.historisches-lexikon-bayerns.de/Lexikon/Geißlerzüge, 17.10.2019, [my translation].

Instead of leading them to rebel against it, their yearning for pressure and submission would be gratified.

Naphta claims that only in his world is there true individuality, because human coexistence is not controlled by a system of values and is therefore chaotic. Consequently the dissolution of individuality through dedication to a higher purpose is experienced as a liberation.

This leads us to the crucial difference between Naphta and Settembrini's understanding of liberty. Whereas in Settembrini's view it is a value approximately equal to self-determination, for Naphta freedom results from casting off the burden of being an individual through abnegation and submission.

In their efforts to convince Hans Castorp, 'life's problem child', of their respective positions, Settembrini and Naphta also argue about other central philosophical terms, and their different conceptions of truth stand out as especially interesting.

Truth

Settembrini´s understanding of truth has its roots in the Renaissance and the Enlightenment. The Renaissance was the cradle of the modern natural sciences with their method of verifying or falsifying hypotheses on the basis of observations in nature or in experiments and thus arriving at verifiable results and well-founded explanations.

In the 18th century, the Age of Enlightenment, human beings were characterized as guided by reason. Correspondingly, the scientific method was esteemed as a means to push back the boundaries of human knowledge and to contribute to the emancipation of human beings from traditional views and beliefs.[25]

---

[25] Lothar Schäfer, ‚Über die Wissenschaft als Muster und als Mittel von Aufklärung' [On science as a model and a method of enlightenment], *Acta Historica Leopoldina*, Nr. 57, 9-23, www.leopoldina.org/uploads/tx_leopublication/Probekapitel_AHL57.pdf

In his ongoing dispute with Naphta Settembrini represents the ideas of the Enlightenment. He has made it his purpose to advance the cause of human progress, the improvement of living conditions through democracy, human rights, education and modern technology. This would be impossible without general consent that by applying the scientific method a shared truth can be established.

> *Do you believe in truth, in objective, scientific truth? That to strive for it is the highest law of morality? That its triumphs over authority are the most moments in the history of the human spirit?!'*
> Chapter 6, 'The City of God and Evil Deliverance', 390.

Only if there is agreement on what can be considered as true, can time-honoured conventions be put under scrutiny. This is the key to social reform and progress and can, of course, also be conducive to a questioning of current hierarchies and privileges. Authorities such as the church and the state can be held to account.

> *Truth and justice are the crown jewels of individual morality; and should a conflict arise with the interests of the state,*

they may very well appear to be hostile to it, but in fact are directed toward the state´s higher, one may even say, transcendent – good.'
Chapter 6: 'The City of God and Evil Deliverance', 392.

While Settembrini emphasizes the liberation of humans through science - 'What about truth, my dear sir, which is so intimately bound up with freedom […]?' (389) - Naphta does not accept a truth independent of one´s world view.

'My good friend,' Naphta replied with sour composure, 'there is no such thing as pure knowledge. The validity of ecclesiastical science – which can be summarized in Saint Augustine´s statement: 'I believe, that I may understand' – is absolutely incontrovertible. Faith is the vehicle of understanding, the intellect is secondary. Your unbiased science is a myth. Faith, a world view, an idea – in short, the will – is always present, and it is then reason´s task to examine and prove it'.
Chapter 6, 390.

By stating that *'there is no such thing as objective knowledge' ('es gibt keine reine Erkenntnis')*, Naphta echoes the philosopher Friedrich Nietzsche´s insight that like perception human thought is dependent on the observer, that is, it is conditioned by social, cultural and biographical factors. The different points of view of various observers on an issue contribute to a nuanced understanding of it.[26]

Naphta, however, is not interested in a complex representation of reality. On the contrary, in his view one's faith takes precedence over knowledge and determines what is true. He illustrates this principle by pointing out that the scientifically verified heliocentric world picture ought to be replaced by the falsified geocentric one, in order to reinstate both Man and God into the positions they are due. Only this world picture communicates that the true purpose of human life lies beyond his/her existence as an individual (598).

Despite its relativist framework, Naphta's world view clearly has its roots in the Middle Ages, as a sculpture in

---

[26] Friedrich Nietzsche, *Genealogie der Moral. Eine Streitschrift.* [*On the Genealogy of Morality: A Polemic.*] 1887, GM III 12, Reclam, 2000, 118.
Michael Tanner, *Nietzsche. A Very Short Introduction.* Oxford University Press, 2000. I used the German translation *Nietzsche.* Freiburg: Herder, 2004, 94.

his room, a gothic Pietà from the 14th century, corrobo-

rates.[27] The findings of the sciences do not have any im-

portance for him, and reason is relegated to the role of

justifying the precepts of the faith (599).

> ,Faith is the vehicle of understanding, the intellect is sec-
> ondary. Your unbiased science is a myth. Faith, a world
> view, an idea – in short, the will – is always present, and it
> is then reason´s task to examine and prove it.' (390)

When subjectivity is taken so far that there is no need

to relate to facts anymore and that any interpretation is

considered as valid, this is tantamount to radical rela-

tivism. The denial of generally accepted criteria for

evaluating the truth is like a licence to spread danger-

ous nonsense and radical thinking.[28]

---

[27] A Pietá is a sculpture of Mary, Mother of God, with the dead Jesus lying
in her lap. In the *Magic Mountain* it does not only relate Naphta's world
view to the Middle Ages, but as an allegorical representation of pain, it is
also a symbol of his world view. Chapter 6, 592.

[28] Erich Fromm (1941) outlines this rhetorical strategy and its dangers in *The
Fear of Freedom*, chapter 7, 'Freedom and Democracy'. 'Another closely related way of discouraging original thinking is to regard all truth as relative.
Truth is made out to be a metaphysical concept, and if anyone speaks about
wanting to discover the truth he is thought backward by the 'progressive'

Naphta himself abuses the insight into the subjectivity of perception in order to legitimize his world view in the same way as this is done by right-wing populist and extremist groups today, when they attempt to make their views acceptable to the public. Thus, it turns out that paradoxically, the ones who ultimately aim at abolishing the plurality of opinions call most clamorously for freedom of expression.

Sacrificed without further ado to that higher idea[29]

Putting the well-being of the community above the interests of the individual is not in itself harmful and can even be beneficial, depending on the specific circumstances and the degree to which this is the case. In

---

thinkers of our age. Truth is declared to be an entirely subjective matter, almost a matter of taste. (214)
[29] Chapter 6, 'Operationes Spirituales', 452.

Naphta´s world, however, the individual is entirely disenfranchised and only extreme experiences like sickness, torture and self-sacrifice endow him or her with dignity.

He [Naphta] ridiculed the philanthropist´s reluctance to shed blood, his reverence for life, claimed that such a reverence for life belonged to only the most banal rubbers-and-umbrellas bourgeois periods ,but that the moment history took a more passionate turn, the moment a single idea, something that transcended mere ,security,' was at work, something suprapersonal, something greater than the individual – and since that alone was a state worthy of mankind, it was, on a higher plane, the normal state of affairs – at that moment, then, individual life would always be sacrificed without further ado to that higher idea, and not only that, but individuals would also unhesitatingly and gladly risk their own lives for it.

Chapter 6, 'Operationes Spirituales', 452.

According to Erich Fromm this view of sacrifice is a hallmark of fascist thinking.

There [in fascism], *sacrifice is not the highest price man may have to pay to assert his self, but it is an aim in itself. This masochistic sacrifice sees the fulfilment of life in its very negation, in the annihilation of the self. It is only the*

supreme expression of what Fascism aims at in all its rami-
fications--the annihilation of the individual self and its ut-
ter submission to a higher power.'
The Fear of Freedom, chapter 7, 'Freedom and Democracy', 231.

The etymology of the term fascism illustrates the insig-

nificance of the individual in fascist organizations and

states.

The word 'fascism' comes from the Latin 'fascis', meaning
'a bundle of rods'. [...] A single rod is very weak, and you
can easily snap it in two. However, once you bundle many
rods together into a fascis, it becomes almost impossible to
break them. This implies that the individual is a thing of no
consequence, but as long as the collective sticks together, it
is very powerful. Fascists therefore believe in privileging the
interests of the collective over those of any individual, [...].
Harari, 340-342.

and

Be particularly careful about the following four words: sac-
rifice, eternity, purity, redemption. If you hear any of these,
sound the alarm. And if you happen to live in a country
whose leader routinely says things like 'Their sacrifice will
redeem the purity of our eternal nation' – know that you are
in deep trouble. Harari, 358.[30]

---

[30] Yuval Noah Harari, *21 Lessons for the 21st century*. London: Random House, 2018. Harari's source is Richard Griffiths, *Fascism*, London: Continuum, 2005, 33. In this context, it is crucial to point to differences in opinion with regard to

With this, Harari warns about fascist political rhetoric. Its constitutive elements can be found in Naphta's thinking, too, although his cause is not the glory of the nation.[31]

There is also a link to the conservative nationalism of the late Wilhelmine Era, the historical period in which the novel is set.[32] Its representatives glorified sacrifice in the name of the people's community based on ethnicity.

The nation that is supposed to identify with the memorial [Monument to the Battle of Nations in Leipzig erected in 1913] is not welded together by culture or faith any more, but by combat, destiny and sacrifice. [...] it is a nation

---

the definition of fascism. Whereas some historians apply the concept only to the original fascist movements and states of the early 20th century, others define it by a set of essential characteristics. This more open definition makes comparison to historically earlier or later movements and ideologies possible. It can also be used as an instrument to identify and clearly label fascist tendencies in current political movements and organizations. Speakers of German can get an impression of the dispute on www.deutschlandfunkkultur.de/debatte-der-umstrittene-begriff-faschismus.976.de.html?dram:article_id=392044 26.7.2017

[31] Developments in the last two decades have shown that religious fundamentalism can be the foundation for fascist organisations, for example jihadist organisations and the Islamic State. Of course, this not limited to Muslim extremism.

[32] The Wilhelmine Era (1890-1914) is the reign of Emperor Wilhelm II, the late phase of the Imperial Era, which began in 1871 with the foundation of the German Empire.

founded on the myth of inwardness and anti-socialist soli-darity. Thomas Nipperdey, S. 143 f.[33]

So it turns out that on the one hand Naphta's thinking has its roots in medieval times, and on the other there are analogies to the nationalist conservatism of the Wilhelmine Era and to fascism, which surfaced in the 1920s. Naphta's world view also includes features of communism consistent with his anti-democratic, anti-liberal ideology. Thus, the resulting theocracy represents tyrannies in general. [34]

---

[33] Thomas Nipperdey, ‚Nationalidee und Nationaldenkmal in Deutschland im 19 Jahrhundert' [Concept of a Nation and National Monument in 19th Century Germany], in: ders., Gesellschaft, Kultur, Theorie. Gesammelte Aufsätze zur neueren Geschichte, Göttingen 1976. I found the quotation in Heinrich August Winkler, *Der lange Weg nach Westen, Deutsche Geschichte I. Vom Ende des Alten Reiches bis zum Untergang der Weimarer Republik.* [Germany: The Long Road West: Volume 1: 1789-1933], München: C.H. Beck, 2000, 324.

[34] As Hanna Arendt demonstrated, authoritarian and totalitarian movements and states share essential elements (Hanna Arendt *The Origins of Totalitarianism,* Schocken Books, 1951).

Lowlands and Highlands

In the novel the world views of the two opponents, Naphta and Settembrini, are also related to spheres of life in the Wilhelmine Era and to rival positions in the contemporary political debate. Hans Castorp himself is an Everyman who is confronted with and caught between them. The narrator of *The Magic Mountain* points out this allegorical dimension.

> *Hans Castorp was neither a genius nor an idiot, and if we refrain from applying the word 'mediocre' to him, we do so for reasons that have absolutely nothing to do with his intelligence and little or nothing to do with his prosaic personality, but rather out of deference to his fate, to which we are inclined to attribute a more general significance.[...]. A human being lives out not only his personal life as an individual, but is also, consciously or subconsciously, an epitome of the lives of his epoch and contemporaries.*
> Chapter 2, At the Tienappels', 30-31.

Settembrini is enthusiastic about the thriving industry and trade, the world of work and business associated with the North German lowlands, Hans Castorp's home. The young man rises in his esteem, when he tells him that he is a ship building engineer. While settling in in Davos, he takes the book *Ocean Steamships* with him on the balcony and he can still wax lyrical about projects like the regulation of the river Elbe, an example of the human and technological progress Settembrini speaks out for.

Whereas in the lowlands, health and progress are paramount, the sanatorium represents a parallel world shaped by illness and looming death. It could be labelled as *decadent* in allusion to the lifestyle associated with fin-de-siècle artists.

While Settembrini hails the advances in the democratization of society in France and Great Britain and regrets that Germany has lagged behind, Naphta's antidemocratic thinking can be found with right-wing conservatives.[35] They exerted their influence to prevent further democratization and liberalization in Germany. Thomas

---

[35] Heinrich August Winkler, *Der lange Weg nach Westen. Deutsche Geschichte I. Vom Ende des Alten Reiches bis zum Untergang der Weimarer Republik.* München: C.H. Beck, 2000, 244-245, 314-315, 322-323.

Mann was an advocate of this German Sonderweg (sep-

arate route). He considered an authoritarian state as nec-

essary to protect German culture.[36] Besides, he sup-

ported the Emperor's war policy previous to and during

World War I.[37]

By 1922, when he gave his speech 'On the German Re-

public', however, he had changed his mind and now ap-

pealed to the German youth to support the Weimar Re-

public. The German liberal democratic state (1918-1933)

was at that time the target of attacks by communists on

the one hand and right-wing conservatives and national

socialists on the other. In the end, it was undermined by

the national socialists, which ultimately led to the Nazi

dictatorship.

In the *Magic Mountain*, published in 1924, Naphta's

theory can be seen as an allusion to both the right-wing

---

[36] Winkler, 340.

[37] Thomas Mann, *Betrachtungen eines Unpolitischen*, Berlin: S. Fischer Verlag. 1918. English Translation: *Reflections of a Nonpolitical Man*, Frederick Ungar Publishing Co, 1983.

conservatism of the pre-war era, the historical setting of the novel, and national socialism, which emerged in the early 1920s, while Mann was finishing his novel. The Naphta chapters point to a high degree of awareness of the implications of the movement and can be read as a warning about its dark sides.

Hans Castorp, who is called 'life's problem child' by Settembrini, proves susceptible to Naphta's ideas. He relates them to life in the sanatorium, his experiences and observations. Naturally, illness, the tuberculosis the patients are there to cure, is at the centre of attention. The protagonist is faced with various stages of suffering, and he also learns to his astonishment that it can be experienced as pleasurable or even lustful. Death is omnipresent, for some a destiny soon to be fulfilled. Every-day life feels like a permanent state of exception. With this closeness to death the rigorous norms and codes of conduct of the Imperial Era, for example with regard to sexuality or the role of women, are not imposed as relentlessly as in the lowlands anymore and can be suspended with impunity. Thus, a sense of freedom in sickness is possible, which, from the point of view of the healthy is judged as decadent, as wantonness and libertinism.

Hans Castorp adapts to this climate and starts a love relationship with the married Madame Chauchat, who is an embodiment of it. That it is an X-ray of her lungs, which he cherishes as a keep-sake of their erotic tête-a-tête and one-night-stand, is a signal of irony. It points to his having merged with the decadent world around him.

So in this world of the sanatorium, liberty is redefined. It is not seen in a hoped-for recovery and the return to the lowlands[38]. On the contrary, it is the escape from the pressures of Wilhelmine bourgeois society, which entails freedom, an escape from the world of duty for middle class men and women, from work and business for the former and for the latter from being practically locked

---

[38] Joachim Ziemßen, Hans Castorp´s cousin, who wants to become an officer in the army, is an exception (582).

up in the home. Of course, this understanding of free-dom implies criticism of the inherently hypocritical society, which was founded on the repression of desire, and thus brought forth the decadent parallel world. [39]

Simultaneously, it is never lost from view that the observed reversal of values, though seemingly harmless at first, is related to Naphta's thinking. The sanatorium is an ideal ecosystem for irrationality, irritation and the eruption of pent-up emotions. Naphta himself points out that his world view thrives best under such conditions (452).[40] In this climate the outbreak of war is celebrated as a release.

---

[39] This included homosexuality, which had repercussions on the author's own life.

[40] There is a correspondence to Sibylle Steinbacher's definition of fascism: [...] they [fascist movements] are tremendously skilled at stirring up passions and banking on emotions, and above all at communicating that a sense of community is valuable for its own sake. Sibylle Steinbacher, www.deutschlandfunkkultur.de/debatte-der-umstrittene-begriff-faschismus.976.de.html?dram:article_id=392044 26.7.2017

A significant object?

However, Hans Castorp does not merge completely with this world, even though the suspension of clock time, which gives life in the lowlands its structure, is an invitation to let himself go. The spatial and temporal removal and gradual alienation make him think about life, and while thus 'playing king', he becomes aware of the dangers of a reversal of humanistic values, such as claimed by Naphta with his apotheosis of illness. His ruminations are expressive of his sincere struggle to find his bearings, which might be an echo of the author's own reflections during the early 1920s.

When listening to the song 'The Linden Tree' Hans Castorp breaks loose of his two teachers. Liberated from their influence he arrives at his own solution. The narrator guides the reader through the listening experience. He warns about the effect the song might have. At first glance, it is just a simple, innocent folk song about a young man feeling homesick. Simultaneously, however, it has the effect of an 'enchantment of the soul with dark consequences' (643).

The linden at the fountain, a paradisaical place, a *locus amoenus*, is a symbol for the speaker's far-away homeland. He remembers happy days there and he is full of nostalgia for it, because life in distant lands is hard ('The cold winds blew' - 'Die kalten Winde bliesen....'). Returning is impossible, because there is more than the miles between him and it. 'Here you'll find your rest.' ('Hier findst du deine Ruh!'), the sure promise at the end of the second stanza turns into 'You would find rest there.' ('Du fändest Ruhe dort.') at the end which is an elliptical conditional sentence. The missing conditional clause 'if ... 'points to an unspoken precondition that precludes the fulfillment of his longing.

The implied conflict can be deduced from the historical context of the song, the restauration period after the Vienna Congress in 1815. In its course the movement for liberty and democratic reforms and the nationalism associated with it were suppressed in order to restore the absolute monarchies in Europe. The crushed hopes of its advocates find expression in the speaker's emotional and spatial distancing from his home country and place of longing. [41]

The narrator in *The Magic Mountain*, however, refers to the later reception history of the song.[42]

> *Let us put it this way: an object created by the human spirit and intellect, that is, a significant object, is 'significant' in that it points beyond itself, is an expression and exponent of a more universal spirit and intellect, of a whole world of feelings and ideas that have found a more or less perfect image of themselves in that object – by which the degree of its significance is then measured* (641).

---

[41] This era was experienced as a political winter in the circle of Franz Schubert's friends. Ian Bostridge *Schubert's Winter Journey. Anatomy of an Obsession*, Faber & Faber, 2015, Chapter 5.

[42] Ian Bostridge works out analogies between *Winter Journey* and *The Magic Mountain* and elaborates on the ambiguity of the lied being both a masterpiece and a folk song. This is important for an understanding of its reception history, which the passage in *The Magic Mountain* is built on. In his interpretation of the role the song plays in *The Magic Mountain* he traces an arc from the death wish of romanticism to national socialism (107-149).

He goes on to establish a connection between the 'world of feelings and ideas' represented by the song and Death, which links it to Naphta's world view and the prototype of a fascist state he envisions as his utopia. Thus, the narrator warns about the dangers of the upcoming national socialism of the early 1920s and simultaneously looks back on right-wing nationalist thinking in the pre-war era with its militarism and imperialism.[43]

One need not be a genius, all one needed was a great deal more talent than the author of this little song about a linden tree to become an enchanter of souls, who would then give the song such vast dimensions that it would subjugate the world. One might even found whole empires upon it, earthly, all-too-earthly empires, very coarse, hailing progress, and, as a matter of fact, not in the least nostalgic, - where the song would decay into some electrical gramophone music. (643)

Although Hans Castorp is clearly susceptible to this dimension of the song, his experiences and reflections enable him to distance himself at least temporarily from

---

[43] Winkler, 310-317.

its temptations. The narrator emphasizes the role of his conscience, which takes over and prevents him from letting himself be drawn into the emotional and ideological abyss. His act of sublimation (triumph over himself, 643) leads to an enhanced, higher kind of love to the song, which is founded on his scruples.

This love remains abstract and elusive if it is not related to Thomas Mann's thinking, in particular the role he attributed to love (in the shape of Eros) in what he conceived of as the ideal political system. At first he discovered it in the nationalist conservative concept of society. But he was wracked by doubts and by and by managed to distance himself. Eventually, he saw it at work in democracy, which he then embraced. [44] There is an analogy between the author's political struggles and Hans Castorp's triumph over himself.

---

[44] Cp. the elaborations on Hans Blüher and Thomas Mann in Dieter Thomä, *Puer robustus. Eine Philosophie des Störenfrieds.* [A Philosophy of the Troublemaker], Berlin: Suhrkamp, 2018, (371-377).

In a previous chapter titled 'Snow' love is actually linked to an ideal image of society. During a ski tour, Hans Castorp liberates himself from the temptations of Death, which in black with a Spanish ruff is a personification of Naphta's world view, and resolves not to let himself be engulfed by it. However, he does not believe that reason, as represented by Settembrini, is strong enough to defeat it. This can only be achieved by the power of love, which is not to be mixed up with lust, because the latter belongs to the realm of death.

Love stands opposed to death – it alone, and not reason, is stronger than death. Only love, and not reason, yields kind thoughts. And form, too, comes only from love and kindness: form and the cultivated manners of a reasonable, genial community and fair commonwealth of men –silently aware of the bloody banquet. (487)

Death and what it stands for still has its attractions, but in the face of the atrocities Hans Castorp witnessed in his dream (485), he makes kindness and charity his ideals. However, this does not signify that he has overcome said temptations for good. Although Settembrini is the one to survive the dispute with Naphta, the increasingly aggressive atmosphere in the sanatorium results from a turning away from value-guided, reasonable behaviour, and finally leads to an eruption of the pent-up passions. The mood in the sanatorium echoes the mood in Wilhelmine society in the run-up to the Great War.

If the protagonist does not lose his composure and takes a moderating, mediating role, this is due to his phlegmatic North German character. Nevertheless, he finally makes the slovenly ways of his fellow-patients his own.

Confusion

In the course of his stay at the Sanatorium Berghof Hans Castorp is increasingly overwhelmed by moral and spiritual confusion. The former is caused by the atmosphere within the sanatorium, the 'emotional circumstances' (675), the latter not least by the ongoing dispute between Settembrini und Naphta. They compete for the prerogative of interpretation of central philosophical terms and deconstruct each other's systems of thought.

Finally, the narrator continues this game in his thoughts and outlines the moot points and contradictions, sometimes assuming the persona of Hans Castorp. Although he concludes that it is all confusion, his line of reasoning suggests that he has not lost his bearings intellectually and that he even enjoys joining in the fray (457-459). He makes clear that a purely rational choice between the two world views is impossible because ultimately, they are political positions and their conversation is a political debate (458). It follows that when Hans Castorp feels closer to Settembrini during his efforts to think independently, he makes an ethical decision and not a rational one. He opts for life instead of death, for philanthropy instead of misanthropy.

Both Settembrini and Naphta like arguing, but Naphta is the one who seeks to confuse more and more actively in the course of the dispute with the aim of questioning basic values guiding human interaction and co-existence. As Settembrini says about Naphta:

His form is logic, but his nature is confusion. (399)

Naphta's monologue about the concepts of 'freedom' and 'revolution' in the context of the nationalist movements of the 19th century mainly serves the purpose of casting doubt on rational argumentation itself (684-686).

Today, Naphta's rhetorical strategies are popular above all with right-wing populist and nationalist movements and parties. They serve their overarching aim to undermine democracy and the rule of law by creating anxiety and confusion in society, not least by questioning and redefining core values of liberal democratic societies. Pointing to the ethical dimension of an issue is mocked or condemned as *moralizing*. Popular strategies of destabilization are the spread of conspiracy theories and of fake news accompanied by a defamation of the so-called *mainstream media* and especially investigative journalism. Their criticism is rejected as fake news, or as a witch hunt.

With reference to freedom of speech and the radically relativist claim that any possible view of a matter is legitimate, not only populists but also lobbyists have cast doubt on peer-reviewed findings of science with the aim to brainwash and manipulate the masses. A prominent example is climate change denial whose advocates have managed to postpone necessary measures and policy changes for decades with increasingly disastrous consequences.

Against this backdrop, the ultimate implications of radical relativism become evident, and it appears that there is wisdom in Settembrini's statement that *'Truth and justice are the crown jewels of individual morality'* (392). Some general consent on how truth can be established is the foundation of a functional society. The plurality of points of view is important and necessary in order to be able to bring about improvements for the common good. The subjectivity of perception in itself is a given, but it can be and has been abused in order to advance self-interest at the expense of everyone else or from a purely destructive motivation.[45] Both kinds of abuse have had dire consequences.

In his most lucid moments Hans Castorp, Everyman and problem child of life, suggests an antidote. So let us listen to him once more, when he says:

> *Love stands opposed to death – it alone, and not reason, is stronger than death. Only love, and not reason, yields kind thoughts.* (487)

---

[45] In Erich Fromm's words: 'There are always groups whose interest is furthered by truth, and their representatives have been the pioneers of human thought; there are other groups whose interests are furthered by concealing truth. Only in the latter case does interest prove harmful to the cause of truth.' Erich Fromm, *The Fear of Freedom*, chapter 7, 'Freedom and Democracy', 214-5.

Love, which is suffused with kindness, is an emotion that reaches out to other humans, or even more generally, to other beings, with the desire to do them good. It can be strong enough to liberate the mind. Mere self-centred or profit-oriented thinking is put on the back burner and the resulting experience is freedom.[46]

---

[46]A comparison with Erich Fromm´s definition of positive freedom suggests itself. Mere negative freedom in the sense of an absence of coercion leads to isolation and anxiety. Only in a state of positive freedom can the individual feel both independent and secure. Positive freedom can be reached through love in the sense of turning towards and accepting others. Erich Fromm, *The Fear of Freedom*, chapter 7, 'Freedom and Democracy'.

VI

Playing along or not – 'Hamlet'

Гамлет

Гул затих. Я вышел на подмостки.
Прислонясь к дверному косяку,
Я ловлю в далеком отголоске,
Что случится на моем веку.

На меня наставлен сумрак ночи
Тысячью биноклей на оси.
Если только можно, Авва Отче,
Чашу эту мимо пронеси.

Я люблю твой замысел упрямый
И играть согласен эту роль.
Но сейчас идет другая драма,
И на этот раз меня уволь.

Но продуман распорядок действий,
И неотвратим конец пути.
Я один, все тонет в фарисействе.
Жизнь прожить - не поле перейти.

Борис Пастернак, (1957)[47]

---

[47] A.Z.Foremanj, http://poemsintranslation.blogspot.com/2015/03/boris-paster-nak-hamlet-from-russian.html

Hamlet

The din has ceased. I enter the stage
While leaning on the post
I capture from the distant echo
What in my time will come to pass.

The dark descends and eyes are focused
through a thousand opera glasses
all at me. Oh, may you, Abba,
let this cup pass from me.

I love your fixed idea,
am willing to take on this role.
Yet, now, another play is staged.
and this time, may you let me go.

The plot, however, is preordained,
And ineluctable the journey's end.
I am alone, all drowns in falsehood.
And Life is not a walk across a field.

Boris Pasternak (1957)[48]

---

[48] Translation by Gudrun Rogge-Wiest and Julia Yakovleva

The speaker of the poem has just gone on the stage in order to play the role of Hamlet in the tragedy by William Shakespeare. In his dual identity as a *dramatis persona* and an actor, a person in his life and times, he takes in the house with its stalls and galleries from the vantage point of a post or column. For the actor the atmosphere in the theatre is vital, as it tells him about the response of the audience and thus about his future life.

With their eyes gazing through opera glasses they seem to him to be keen observers who are not only interested in his acting, but also in him as a person. The lighting with its focus on the stage leaves them in the shadows, so that their faces are unrecognizable. This constellation is reminiscent of a surveillance situation with its sinister atmosphere and threatening overtones.[49]

Given the socio-historical context of the Soviet Union, Pasternak´s poem can be interpreted as a dramatization

---

[49] It evokes the concept of the panopticon designed by the English philosopher Jeremy Bentham (1748-1832) with the purpose of achieving maximum efficiency in surveillance in prisons.

of the position of the individual in a totalitarian state. Like an actor the individual plays the role ascribed to him or her. Deprived of the freedom of speech and of self-determination he realizes that his future is preordained, which is not to say that it cannot suddenly be rewritten in mid-action due to the arbitrariness of autocratic rule.

In Shakespeare's *Hamlet* the protagonist is likewise faced with demands to play certain roles, and he pauses to check out the implications first and to set a trap of his own. He hesitates to fulfil his father's command to take revenge and contrives to escape his uncle's plot to murder him. In the end, however, he consents against his better judgment to play his part in a court entertainment staged by his uncle, in the course of which he is fatally injured. It almost seems that in the end he has no real choice whether to play along or not. The prince's fate is not in his own hands.

In Pasternak's poem the Hamlet actor and speaker's agony finds expression in the invocation 'Abba, let this cup pass from me', the words of Jesus Christ, another son who has doubts about the role assigned to him by his father. The quote is from the Gospel of Matthew, chapter 26, which relates Christ's experiences in the garden of Gethsemane. Jesus pleads with his father to release him from their covenant, but finally yields knowing that he can't escape his destiny and that a traitor is close by waiting to deliver him to the authorities. The reader gets very close to Christ's experience of great fear, reluctance and finally resignation.

The existential situation of being at the mercy of a higher power is at the core of both the poem, Shakespeare's play and the passage from the Gospel. Whereas Jesus can be confident that his sacrifice has a purpose and that he'll ascend and sit beside God as his son, there is no redemption for the speaker. Instead the plot ends with the consolidation of autocratic power propped up by contemporaries, who might be eager to denounce any divergent behavior to the regime.

Julian Barnes quotes Pasternak´s poem 'Hamlet' in *The Noise of Time*, his fictional biography of the Russian composer Shostakovich published in 2016. It is told from the point of view of Shostakovich but in the third person[50] with the composer´s relationship to the Soviet state under Stalin and later under Khrushchev as its predominant theme. *The Noise of Time* deals with the experience of collaborating under the constant threat of attracting the displeasure of the authorities. Acting against his conscience by making concessions, Shostakovich was so humiliated that living was an agony and death seemed preferable.

'He knew he would be allowed to live, and receive the best medical attention. But, in a way, that was worse. Because it is always possible to bring the living to a lower point. You cannot say that of the dead.' (135)

---

[50] The narrative mode is free indirect discourse.

'And this, perhaps, was their final triumph over him. Instead of killing him, they had allowed him to live, and by allowing him to live, they had killed him. This was the final, unanswerable irony of his life: that by allowing him to live, they had killed him.' (177)

When there is no freedom of expression and when the state ropes art in and misuses it as a propaganda tool, it can still become a vehicle of resistance as in Boris Pasternak's public readings of Shakespeare's Sonnet 66:

When Pasternak read Sonnet 66 in public, the audience would wait keenly through the first eight lines, eager for the ninth:
And art made tongue-tied by authority.
At which point they would join in – some under their breath, some whisperingly, the boldest among them fortissimo, but all giving the lie to that line, all refusing to be tongue-tied.
Barnes, 93-94.

According to Barnes, Shakespeare's plays Hamlet and Macbeth were considered as potentially subversive.

,But even more than poetry, tyrants hated and feared the theatre. Shakespeare held a mirror up to nature, and who could bear to see their own reflection? So Hamlet was banned for a long time; Stalin loathed the play almost as much as he loathed Macbeth.' (88)

The dictator could not help but compare himself with the kings represented in these tragedies. Neither was in any way a flattering image of a ruler. In both plays, the king has come to power by means of regicide, plots murders to consolidate his rule and is killed in the end. The spectators could recognize in them traits of their own rulers, and the indirect criticism likely induced a grim sense of satisfaction. Thus, these old texts were able to communicate over a distance of approximately 350 years and to produce a cathartic effect. Pasternak´s poem is an allusion to this experience. Due to the socio-political circumstances, however, speaker has even less room for manoeuver than Shakespeare´s Hamlet.

VII

The western *High Noon* – a wakening call

When you watch the four outlaws finally swaggering through the streets of the small frontier town Hadley-ville, you'll have lived through sixty minutes of suspense during which the town marshal has tried in vain to rally support to fight them. Although the western *High Noon*, which was directed by Fred Zinnemann, is more than sixty years old[51], it has never ceased to be up-to-date. It is a fascinating film not least because it illustrates perfectly the threat to a community posed by a coming to power of populist leaders and authoritarian rulers. What is more, it asks the vital question who will rise to defend the rule of law in a liberal democratic society. The disturbing answer of this film is that not many citizens

---

[51] It was released in 1952.

are able or willing to do so. Too many have stopped appreciating it and they don't seem to be aware of the consequences of their indifference.

Hadleyville is on the New Mexico territory. It is the late 19th century. Frank Miller, a convicted murderer was released from a prison in one of the Northern States of the US in spite of a death sentence and is about to arrive in the town at noon. On hearing this news, Will Kane, who resigned from his office as the town Marshal earlier in the day, returns to pin on the tin star again and to gather together a posse to protect the town against Miller.

While the hands of the clock move steadily and relentlessly from ten fifty towards noon and the expected violent confrontation, the camera follows Kane around town in what is almost real time introducing representatives of various social groups to the viewer and giving an insight into their personalities and mindsets.

It is the shocking outcome of Kane's quest that neither in the streets nor in their homes nor in the church nor in the saloon is he able to make men commit themselves to his cause. They refuse to support the Marshal for a variety of motives. Some are simply scared for their lives. The bartender in the saloon and his customers, however, come out in favour of Miller. The bartender gleefully anticipates Kane's death and his customers are laughing in the Marshal's face and hailing a new dawn. So is the owner of the hotel who expects his business to revive after Miller's return. Obviously, Miller gains popular support by the mere presence of his gang even before his arrival and although his sidekicks are undoubtedly villains.

The judge, who convicted Miller and who like Kane embodies the law, leaves town. He does not only take his law books with him, but also the scales, symbol of justice, and the American flag. While packing his things, he compares the impending situation with the return of a tyrant to Athens around 500 BC. Although the Greeks had banished him because he had made their life hell, they let him invade the city on his return with an army and 'stood by while he executed members of the legal government'. The allusion is strong evidence that the plot can be interpreted as an allegory of the threat posed by an aspiring tyrant to a civilized community that is not willing or able to prevent his rise to power.

In the church some speakers make a strong case for putting up resistance. They argue that the town has been a safe place for women and children since Miller was put behind bars. The law with Marshal Kane as its representative has protected them effectively.

The proponents of defence are trumped, however, by those who are reluctant to fight or even explicitly speak out against Kane's mission. The most eloquent speaker is a leading townsman, who claims that potential investors from the North might lose interest if the news of a shootout with Miller spread. He maintains that Miller only seeks to revenge himself on Kane, so the problem would be solved if the marshal left the town. Those who support him either underestimate the danger or they have come to the conclusion that the Marshal's resignation as well as the law's hasty retreat in the person of the Judge actually serve their interests. It seems that a number of citizens who pull the strings behind the scenes are eager to clear the way for a new era because they expect to benefit from the chaos and upheaval Miller's presence would cause in the town. They do not only believe that if they left him alone he would leave them unscathed, but that like him they could break the law with impunity, as well.

Having failed to rally support Kane prepares to take on Miller and his gang single-handedly not only because the confrontation is ultimately inescapable but also because he has made the defence of the rule of law in the town his mission. Thus he does not arrest Miller's associates preemptively before his arrival given that they have not broken the law so far. When the bandits seek him out in the end, he only shoots them in self-defence, whereas Miller has come to execute those who rightfully detained and convicted him. That Kane does not lay claim to power after the shootout is further evidence that he does not embody authoritarian leadership.

The director of the film, Fred Zinnemann, supports this view in his autobiography:[52]

It was a story of a man who must make a decision according to conscience. His town – symbol of a democracy gone soft – faces a horrendous threat to its people's way of life. Determined to resist, and in deep trouble, he moves all over the place looking for support but finding there is nobody who will help him; each has a reason for not getting involved. In the end he must meet his chosen fate all by himself, his town's doors and windows firmly locked against him ... It is a story that still happens everywhere, every day.
Zinnemann, Fred (1992), *An Autobiography,* London: Bloomsbury. 97.

---

[52] The context of the 1950s suggested a variety of allegorical readings, such as Kane standing for the USA as a superpower defying communism, or the film criticizing the activities of the House Un-American Activities Committee during the McCarthy era. Phillip Drummond, *Zwölf Uhr Mittags. Mythos und Geschichte eines Filmklassikers*. Europa Verlag Hamburg/Wien, 1997, 99-100; 110-12.

Regardless of Kane's exact role, it would be interesting to know how affairs in the town would have developed if Kane had not killed the four outlaws. The conduct of Frank Miller's gang does not make it hard to guess. In their search for Kane they count on the rule of law being suspended and exercise the law of the strongest demolishing property at will.

Besides, studies on the success of populist movements in democracies and the emergence of authoritarian regimes can complete the picture. In her famous study, Hannah Arendt has worked out that the liberal democratic Weimar Republic in Germany (1919 – 1933) practically abolished itself allowing that its democratic institutions were undermined.[53] As illustrated in the film such developments are viable only with popular support. The

---

[53] Hannah Arendt (1951) *The Origins of Totalitarianism.* I used the German edition *Elemente und Ursprünge totaler Herrschaft*, 13. Auflage 2009, 659.

people either do not resist the changes or they even consent to the restriction of civil liberties and the suspension of the rule of law.

In order to establish power and to consolidate it, the rulers have to create bogeymen. Certain minorities are discriminated against or made into the target of popular resentment. In the end, the community is divided into the movement's followers, the people, and others, who are vilified as the enemy of the people. Hannah Arendt explains why it is often one's best friends who become denunciators (Arendt, 696-7). Thus, the citizens contribute to developments that are ultimately against their own interests because they lead to arbitrary and oppressive rule. Arbitrariness is a constitutive element of authoritarian regimes as it keeps people in a permanent state of uncertainty and mutual distrust, which stabilizes the regime.

By pointing out the dangers of political apathy and disenchantment *High Noon* can serve as a wakening call for the citizens of liberal democracies all over the world.

By the way, Kane is only able to win the final shootout because his wife supports him on an equal footing.

VIII

Pockets full and empty – Lord Ribbeck of Ribbeck

Herr von Ribbeck auf Ribbeck

Herr von Ribbeck auf Ribbeck im Havelland,
Ein Birnbaum in seinem Garten stand,
Und kam die goldene Herbsteszeit
Und die Birnen leuchteten weit und breit,
Da stopfte, wenn's Mittag vom Turme scholl,
Der von Ribbeck sich beide Taschen voll,
Und kam in Pantinen ein Junge daher,
So rief er: ‚Junge, wiste 'ne Beer?'
Und kam ein Mädel, so rief er: ‚Lütt Dirn,
Kumm man röwer, ick hebb 'ne Birn.'

So ging es viel Jahre, bis lobesam
Der von Ribbeck auf Ribbeck zu sterben kam.
Er fühlte sein Ende. 's war Herbsteszeit,
Wieder lachten die Birnen weit und breit;
Da sagte von Ribbeck: ‚Ich scheide nun ab.
Legt mir eine Birne mit ins Grab.'
Und drei Tage drauf, aus dem Doppeldachhaus,
Trugen von Ribbeck sie hinaus,
Alle Bauern und Büdner mit Feiergesicht
Sangen ‚Jesus meine Zuversicht'[54],

---

[54] Easter hymn. The lyrics is attributed to Luise Henriette, Electress of Brandenburg (1627-1667). It was set to music by Johann Crüger, 1592-1662 and published in Christoph Runge's *Geistliche Lieder und Psalmen* (Berlin, 1653).

Und die Kinder klagten, das Herze schwer:
‚He is dod nu. Wer giwt uns nu 'ne Beer?'

So klagten die Kinder. Das war nicht recht -
Ach, sie kannten den alten Ribbeck schlecht;
Der neue freilich, der knausert und spart,
Hält Park und Birnbaum strenge verwahrt.
Aber der alte, vorahnend schon
Und voll Mißtraun gegen den eigenen Sohn,
Der wußte genau, was damals er tat,
Als um eine Birn' ins Grab er bat,
Und im dritten Jahr aus dem stillen Haus
Ein Birnbaumsprößling sproßt heraus.

Und die Jahre gingen wohl auf und ab,
Längst wölbt sich ein Birnbaum über dem Grab,
Und in der goldenen Herbsteszeit
Leuchtet's wieder weit und breit.
Und kommt ein Jung' übern Kirchhof her,
So flüstert's im Baume: ‚Wiste 'ne Beer?'
Und kommt ein Mädel, so flüstert's: ‚Lütt Dirn,
Kumm man röwer, ick gew' di 'ne Birn.'

So spendet Segen noch immer die Hand
Des von Ribbeck auf Ribbeck im Havelland.

Theodor Fontane (1889)[55]

[55] *Deutsche Gedichte. Eine Anthologie*, Reclam, 2000, 223.

Lord Ribbeck of Ribbeck

Lord Ribbeck of Ribbeck in Havelland,
And in his garden a pear tree would stand.
When autumn steeped all in its golden light
The pears were shining far and wide.
Whenever the bells of the tower struck noon
He crammed both pockets with pears anon.
He called: would you like a pear, my lad?'
When in his clogs a boy passed by
And when it was a girl, he called: My lass,
I ´ve got a pear, come nigh.

It went on thus for many a year
Until Lord Ribbeck´s end came near.
He felt he ´d pass, it was autumn, again,
And far and wide the pears were laughing;
It was then that Ribbeck said, I´m dying,
Put a pear into this grave of mine.
And three days later Lord Ribbeck was moved,
Out of the house with the half-hipped roof.
With solemn faces cottagers and peasants
Sang Jesus Christ, my sure defence.

And the children moaned with their hearts full of cares:
He is dead, now. Who is going to give us our pears?
So the children moaned. This was not fair -
O, they were far from getting his measure.
The new one, though, he pinches his penny
and strictly shuts off the park and the pear-tree.
However, all but trusting his son
With a sense of foreboding, the older man
knew well what he was doing when
he asked for a pear in his grave back then.
When three years had passed, from this house so quiet
the shoot of a pear tree saw the light.

Again the years have come and gone,
a pear tree has hung over the grave for long,
And in the golden autumn light
again it's shining far and wide.
And in the tree it whispers: ... a pear, my lad?
when through the churchyard a boy comes by
and when it is a girl, it whispers: Lass,
I've got a pear, come nigh.

And thus Lord Ribbeck of Ribbeck 's hand
is still a blessing in Havelland.

Theodor Fontane (1889)

Theordor Fontane modelled his ballad Lord Ribbeck of Ribbeck (Herr von Ribbeck) on Hans Georg von Ribbeck (1689-1759), a squire in Havelland, a region west of Berlin, which was a part of Prussia at that time. Today it lies in the German state of Brandenburg.[56]

It is a sign of Ribbeck´s benevolence that he gives away pears from his tree to children in the neighbourhood. I imagine him to be similar to Lord Grantham in the film series Downton Abbey, a well-meaning patriarch, who runs the family property responsibly and treats his employees and tenants fairly, but who does not fundamentally question the social hierarchy of the four estates of the realm, from which his privileged position originates.

When he dies he is racked by doubts whether his son is going to be a caring patriarch like him. As a pre-emptive measure he asks for a pear to be buried with him. In fact, with his son taking charge of the estate it becomes

---

[56] de.wikipedia.org/wiki/Hans_Georg_von_Ribbeck. The manor house on the official website (www.von ribbeck.de) of the estate, was built in the 19th century.

clear, how precarious the situation of the poorer population is when their well-being depends on the good-will of the landlord.

Old Lord Ribbeck's plan implemented at the very last moment suggests a more sustainable model of participation in wealth. A pear tree grows out of the pear in his grave, and the children are again offered the fruits. This time they can pick them themselves. However, he has taken this measure so late that the children have to wait for some years until the new tree carries pears. This gap in the supply points to the power relations behind the apparently idyllic first impression. Charity is not obligatory for the nobility. It is an act of generosity a lord of the manor can afford to make, and even though it is a kind gesture, it is still an element of arbitrary rule. If the squire is charitable, he is esteemed for it in society. Charity can even be considered a smart policy, because it is perpetuated by gratefulness and subjugation of its beneficiaries.

But if he decides not to be generous, his position nevertheless remains unquestioned.

Old Lord Ribbeck´s benevolence is not just a personal trait. It arises from the spirit of his times, the 18th century. Then, emotions were discovered as a source for the moral consciousness of human beings.[57] In a countermovement to the rationalism of the 17th century, loving care and charity became central literary themes and took root as social values. In this context old Lord Ribbeck embodies an ideal, which has certainly had its representatives in life. With his selfishness and his avarice his son is his counter-image, a personality type, whose behavior

---

[57] *Deutsche Literatur in Schlaglichtern*, Bernd Balzer und Volker Mertens, Eds., Mannheim: Meyers Lexikonverlag, 1990, S. 201 ff.
The English authors Anthony A. Earl of Shaftesbury (1621-1683) and Francis Hutcheson (1694-1746) outlined the theory of moral sense. *'Hutcheson argues frequently and forcefully that we are capable of irreducibly benevolent affections and passions, against the view he associates with Hobbes and Mandeville that all passions are, in the final analysis, forms of self-interest. Self-interest, he maintains, cannot explain why we approve what we do, and in particular, why we identify with those of benevolent character.'* Francis Hutcheson on the Emotions (1694-1746), *Supplement to 17th and 18th Century Theories of Emotions*, Amy M. Schmitter, Stanford Encyclopaedia of Philosophy, 2010, plato.stanford.edu/entries/emotions-17th18th/LD7Hutcheson.html.

demonstrates what the situation can be like as well due to the power relations in an estates-based society.

The comparison between the two generations of Ribbecks can be interpreted as implied criticism of the social and political conditions during the era in which the ballad was composed.[58] The sequence of temporary liberalization, as during the Revolution of 1848, and subsequent restoration was painfully familiar to the author Theodor Fontane. He had to endure the authoritarian, estates-based Prussian state. While being in its service, he was not only financially dependent on it, but he was humiliated by its austerity, its arbitrariness and the pressure to adhere to its ideological precepts. Despite writing for the nationalist conservative paper 'Kreuzzeitung',

---

[58] My source for this is *Fontane. Ein Jahrhundert in Bewegung*. Hamburg: Rowohlt Verlag, 2. Auflage, Februar 2019, by Iwan-Michelangelo D'Aprile. The author concludes that analogies in Fontane's ballads work as a vehicle for criticism. Allusions to the reign of Frederick the Great (Friedrich der Große, 1740-1786), for example, were a popular device used by contemporary authors to convey criticism of the authoritarian state (144, 156-158). Besides, Fontane used the stuff of legend and history as a frame of reference as well as his own observations during his stays in Great Britain, which at that time was more liberal and progressive than Prussia.

which represented the interests of the nobility and the court, he was critical of the social and political system and open to modernization in all areas of life.[59] He perused the newspapers daily over decades and very likely observed with interest the emergence of the labour movement and the beginnings of a welfare state in Germany after 1871. His own precarious situation can serve as evidence that social legislation makes sense. In fact, it is invaluable, because it makes state support for those who have become destitute through illness or through accidents at work legally binding.

So criticism of contemporary Prussia is certainly implied in Fontane's ballad as is a dream of wellbeing for all. Nevertheless, aristocrat as he may be, old Lord Ribbeck has remained a model for human kindness and compassion.

---

[59] This is particularly evident in his own fields of expertise: the press, literature and the theatre.

Epilogue

Nevertheless be free is the title of this collection of essays, and freedom is indeed the overarching theme. It is not freedom in the sense of absence of coercion, but an inner freedom, which can be reached by leaving fears and prejudices behind. Harry Potter standing by Hagrid and not letting himself be manipulated by Voldemort is an illustration of this. He knows Hagrid well and is therefore not susceptible to slander against his friend. His friendship defies any false suspicions. Gregor in *Sansibar or The Last Reason* works up the courage to free himself from his party obligations and to give his life a new purpose, which empowers him and helps him to cope with the looming challenges.

Once attained, this inner freedom does not remain uncontested. On the contrary, it is jeopardized by inner and outer influences. Hans Castorp in *The Magic Mountain*, for instance, is exposed to Settembrini and Naphta´s philosophizing as well as to the atmosphere in the sanatorium. However, he uses his free time for reflection, and in his best moments he temporarily arrives at independent views. Although he ultimately lacks the energy to resist the spirit of the times, his conscious decision for love and kindness arising from a vision of humans coexisting happily and peacefully indicates that in these moments of inner freedom he considers the well-being of others, too.

In *High Noon* Marshal Will Kane is the target of Miller´s revenge, because he represents the rule of law, which protects equal rights and the dignity of all members of the community against the law of the strongest. Will´s determination is the result of a conscious ethical decision. Therefore, he does not let himself be misled by his fellow-citizens playing down the imminent danger. His inner freedom becomes evident, when he resists all the attempts to keep him from confronting Miller.

Inner freedom is much harder to achieve, when society as a whole does not orient itself by humanistic values, when outer freedom is limited, when freedom of opinion, freedom of the press and the independence of the judiciary are restricted or even suspended. Still, the speaker in Heinrich Heine's poem 'All Enshrouded in Grey Clouds' finds refuge from political oppression and uncertainty in an ironical reflection of contemporary circumstances. In contrast, Pasternak's speaker in 'Hamlet' does not have any room for manoeuver. The surveillance by the totalitarian state haunts the mind, as well. There is no refuge, not even in irony. So in Pasternak's poem there is only the yearning for freedom and the desperation of being trapped.

When someone has to struggle for the day-to-day survival of themselves and their family, be it because of political uncertainty or economic hardships, there is little room for fundamental philosophical reflections. The best foundation for a free life is a liberal, democratic society with the rule of law and a strong welfare state. A good education and a certain economic independence are favourable conditions for humans to realize inner freedom. A free person does not fall into an obsession easily. Nor do they make a narrative so much their own that they are unable to bear any questioning of it. With inner freedom comes distrust of radical positions that are incompatible with humanistic values and the ability to distance oneself from them.

Despite favourable conditions it remains hard enough to emancipate oneself from influences and to find one's own position. The issues are complex and require weighing competing interests. What does a good balance between economic freedom and social security, between a functioning economy and the protection of the environment and the climate look like? What changes are necessary to enable all people on earth to have a good life?

It should not be overlooked that a sense of freedom can also arise from doing without something and from refraining from doing something. This extends to not wielding one's power to the utmost, to not playing hardball to defend our interests. In this way both individuals and in particular lobbyists from industry, agriculture or the world of finance could make a big difference, because their behaviour has a great impact on the future of the whole society and ultimately of all inhabitants of the earth. The ideal of sustainability established with the ratification of the Kyoto Protocol in 1992 is a reasonable guideline. It is based on the precept that all costs, including environmental and social ones have to be considered in economic calculations.

Even though the old Lord Ribbeck in 'Lord Ribbeck of Ribbeck' did not mean to reform the society of his time, he looked beyond the horizon of his estate. He was not trapped in self-interest. His kindness made him care for other people and to take action to improve their lives.

The central metaphor of the poem, the planting of a pear-tree, is expressive of the desire to enable all children to have a good life. It is also a beautiful image for a more sustainable economy.

The middle classes of the world are today's elites. With regard to numbers there is great potential to bring about change. However, like the young Lord Ribbeck, we are trapped far too often in our own worlds and only think of our own advancement instead of rearranging our priorities and spending our joint energies in planting enough pear trees for the generations of children to come.